STEPTOE BUTTE

STEPTOE BUTTE

POEMS

BILL SIVERLY

Windfall Press • Portland, Oregon

Steptoe Butte is published in an edition of 350 and is sold by independent bookstores in Oregon. Order by US mail or online at:

Windfall Press
PO Box 19007
Portland, Oregon 97280-0007

www.windfalljournal.com

Cover photo: "Steptoe Butte in October" by Bill Siverly
Author photo: Jutta Donath
Book Design: Cheryl McLean

Siverly, Bill 1943–
    Steptoe Butte: poems / Bill Siverly
Library of Congress Control Number: 2012953409
ISBN: 978-0-9700302-4-5

Printed in the United States of America.

This book is printed on acid-free paper.

Acknowledgments

Thanks to the publications in which versions of these poems first appeared:

Cloudbank: "Garden in Winter"

Fault Lines: "Inheritance"

Moving Mountain: "Rock"

Northwind Anthology 2008: "Cathlapotle"

poetry.us.com (online): "Replanting Peas," "Garden in Winter"

Windfall: *A Journal of Poetry of Place*: "Lownsdale Square," "Cathlapotle," "Turning Compost," "Fish Creek," "Death and the Mother," "Wind Mountain," "Big Hole," "The House on Lancaster Road," "Julia and the Salmonberries," "Widow-Maker," "Green Chain," "The Best Days," "Perfectly Still"

Writing Nature 2010 (online): "Agriculture"

Thanks for the close reading and ongoing discourse that made these poems possible: Jutta Donath, Barbara Drake, Michael McDowell, Joseph Stroud, and Mike Wiley.

Thanks to past and present members of our poetry group: Alison Apotheker, Tim Applegate, Jessica Lamb, Michael McDowell, and Amy Minato. Thanks to the poets of Poetry Church.

Contents

Preface

Some words about the formal intentions of the book may be in order. All of the poems of *Steptoe Butte* but one follow a twenty-one line form developed from the orally based poetry of Northwest Native American mythtellers, ancient Greek epic, and Roman written poetry. The form consists of four stanzas of four lines each, plus a middle stanza of five lines. The middle line of the middle stanza contains the central idea, value, theme, image, or metaphor that animates the poem.

Parallelism defines the structure, not in terms of meter and rhyme, but in terms of what Robert Bringhurst in speaking of Haida mythtelling calls "thematic parallelism." Stanza one is parallel to stanza five in terms of meaning, theme, imagery, analogy, or sometimes simply by repetition of words or grammar. Stanza two is parallel to stanza four in similar fashion. Sometimes the first two lines of the middle stanza parallel the last two, framing the important middle line between them. And sometimes the middle line itself is balanced by means of chiasmus, a grammatical arrangement in two or more parallel parts.

The fundamental principle of such a structure is balance. A poem could end where it began, or lead to a complete reversal of where it began. Everything leads up to and away from the middle line, which serves as a pivot for the whole poem. "Parallel" can mean not only similarity, but also antithesis. For ancient orally based cultures, the story of things getting out of balance and balance being restored was the essential story. Nature always brings things back into balance.

Parallelism structures each poem and the book as a whole. The one poem different from others is "Steptoe Butte," the middle poem of the book. Its seven stanzas lead up to and away from the middle stanza, whose middle line becomes in the broadest sense the central theme of the book.

As the poems lead up to and away from "Steptoe Butte," they form a kind of "mountain." The following balanced table of contents may help clarify this structure, as well as indicate which poem can be found opposite a poem on the "other side of the mountain." Balance is not a feature of our culture today, and restoring it to lyric poetry seems appropriate. The sound of the mountain resonates through time.

Bill Siverly, Portland, Oregon

Balanced Table of Contents

Each poem parallels another poem, from the Prelude and Envoi at the foot of
the mountain to the title poem at the summit.

Prelude: Inheritance

for Barbara Drake

The Siverly farm lay on a flood plain between the Iowa and Mississippi,
rich bottom land near the village of Oakville, where my father was born.
Uncle Dwight took over raising corn after his siblings had gone
to other lives in Idaho, San Francisco, Wapello, and Muscatine.

I remember Uncle Dwight teaching me to shuck corn, and waking me
at five a.m. for milking chores, showing the town kid how to grasp
and tug the teats, the splat of milk hitting the bucket, my head leaning
against the warm sides of cows, whose stoic patience filled the barn.

I remember hogs grunting at the trough, and chickens and lots of cats.
No horses anymore—instead a bumpy ride on a tractor.
But most of all I recall the sound an owl made in the towering oak
above the cicada-buzzing, cricket-chirping porch at dusk.
Aunt Eileen said it was a screech owl, as it trilled in the humid night.

Dwight's son was killed in Viet Nam, his daughter married
and moved away. After Eileen died, Dwight retired to Wapello
and put that rich bottom land near Oakville up for sale. Someone paid
top dollar to grow more lucrative soy on land long known for corn.

In Oregon with my dead father's subdivided share of the sale,
I started Windfall Press, home to poems that linger in us,
like yours about lambs and roosters on your Lilac Hill farm near Yamhill,
the one about the owl that died, the one about the owl you set free.

Temenos

for Jutta Donath

After the chaos and grief of our double divorces,
after the death of Dieter and dissolution of his estate,
his widow Ingrid sitting alone in darkened rooms,
we clattered into Görlitz to be married once again.

We found our refuge in the village church at Weinhübel,
its cool musty stones laid down in 1337,
when every Mass spoken within these foursquare walls
glowed with presence human and divine.

Having certified we had been baptized in good faith,
the pastor stood before us on a sun-ripened August morning.
Ein Schmetterling fluttered into church and circled us once,
hovered near the vase of radiant sunflowers,
danced down the aisle and out the open door.

Cloudy windows of Weinhübel's Church of the Resurrection,
its carved flaming heart perched on a newel,
its golden angel bearing a font that could be raised or lowered,
bestowed a glow that confirmed us in our love.

It was 1989, the year the Wall came down.
Ingrid moved to Berlin in search of a new beginning.
We keep looking for that butterfly passing through.
It circled us once, then vanished into the years.

Remission

for Jutta Donath

At the end of December, New Year's fog drips into your arm.
A rustle of cold rain begins outside the barrier brain.
The nightwatch changes shifts and begins its tour of arteries.
They try every knob in your chest to see which doors are locked.

As chemicals slaughter legions of lymphoma,
free radicals threaten muscles around your heart.
Blood struggles to supply red cells and white cells.
A headache hee-haws like a black maria siren lasting days.

Ghosts steal your hair like white men stealing land.
Visible lumps withdraw from your shoulders and arms.
You begin to imagine that you will break free.
You want to live again in your own skin and bones and hair,
though the shadow of dispossession lingers in your blood.

Security breaks down doors and hauls away the few
Black Bloc cells hiding behind the body's internal night.
The headache fades like a Doppler shift and stops.
Suddenly everything is quiet, too quiet to believe.

The violence of the cure means it's working, doctors say.
After the last infusion, doctors order PET scans.
Lymphoma, they say, has entered a dark phase, like the moon.
Awakened from the fear of death, you open doors and live.

The House on Lancaster Road

Blackberry vines, broken laurel, and Scotch broom
surround the peeling house set on a slope above the road.
Built in '53, added onto in '74, the place has seen three families
passing through like generations of crows and blue jays.

Tall firs and cedars shadow the roof, and moss grows deep.
An ancient pear tree still bears fruit, or it doesn't.
One year a young man drives up to call on the woman living there.
He sees what needs to be cleared away and built.

They inhabit the house together, and smoke rises like the moon.
The pendulums of antique clocks swing more slowly here.
Dwelling there is who they are, and they are always learning to dwell
in this house, to occupy its wooden bed, table, and chairs.
They stoke a hearth where bitter winter branches burn.

In March the old man spades and rakes to build
mounds of composted earth to host lettuce and potatoes.
The woman delights in growing things and plants
seeds of cosmos that will tickle the blooming granddaughter.

One year the rain will find them gone. The garden
will go back to blackberry vines, broken laurel, and Scotch broom.
The energy of God, coiled in dark earth,
awaits the human work of care to spiral into waiting sky.

The Clearing

Breaching dense forest on the west side of the Willamette,
travelers beached their canoes and cleared an acre of underbrush
to make a camp, a place to rest, a place to die when disease
cleared Kalapuya towns in 1833.

Ten years later William Overton, hitching a ride upriver
in Asa Lovejoy's big canoe, said he was getting sick
and besides, Lovejoy should see the best potential claim
along the whole Willamette, already half-cleared for use.

Only a few maples and oaks left at the edge of a forest,
the river ran deep enough for deep-draft ships,
shady birthplace of the future, the generation of money.
Lovejoy filed for Overton and himself a homestead claim:
640 acres for a twenty-five-cent filing fee.

Eventually Overton tired of felling trees and building roads,
sold his half a claim to Francis Pettygrove for fifty dollars,
and lit out for Texas, where some say he was hanged.
Pettygrove built a store at the future corner of First and Washington.

Lovejoy sold his half a claim to Benjamin Stark for some cattle
and twelve hundred dollars, moved back home to Oregon City.
A few Kalapuya set up wigwams along the forest edge of town,
and soon they followed their ancestors into the shadows.

Bonneville Dam in Winter

At Cottonwood Point, where Lewis and Clark once camped,
Clark County has anchored replica canoes.
Alex and Emma jump into the one with fiberglass salmon,
imagine themselves paddling upstream.

At the Cascade town site Tom McNatt built his stable and hotel,
long gone and overgrown with ferns and osoberry.
McNatt's lone grave fascinates Alex,
who stands on the fence and reads the stone aloud.

Looming behind a curtain of spillway mist,
its concrete face pitted and dappled with moss,
Bonneville Dam was built to last a century or so.
Grandfather says, "It's only six years older than me,
and when it's gone, you will see Columbia's cascades."

The blockhouse at Fort Rains eventually fell
when the river undercut the bank.
Above the dam Lake Bonneville begins,
and day-dreaming Emma launches a fresh canoe.

Lewis and Clark did not stop at Little White Salmon,
but next to the hatchery Alex and Emma throw snow.
Then they lie down in the car, drifting downstream,
shooting immortal rapids in their dreams.

Cathlapotle

for Mike Wiley

As long as oil from distant lands
can still deliver us to destinations on demand,
we drive the Range Rover north to Ridgefield,
three thousand folks in eight hundred homes.

Many commute by asphalt to Vancouver,
some from mass-produced gingerbread mansions
sited on the ridge like churches of money
overlooking wildlife and wetlands far below.

Overlooking the plank house reconstructed there,
we enter the circular doorway to a dim interior world:
eighty feet of living space along a central fire pit,
carved house posts of ancestors looming at the back,
sliding planks overhead venting smoke from ancient fires.

Homeward bound, Lewis and Clark camped the night
where three rivers merge, where Cathlapotle
made their way by swift canoe through rich
spirit worlds of Salmon, Blue Jay, Elk, and Wapato.

Nine hundred Cathlapotle by Clark's count
dwelled in fourteen plank lodges.
Suddenly we realize, when all the oil is gone,
everyone we know will live in one room.

The Best Days

The sweetest job I ever had was restoring phone line
from somewhere east of Bovil, cross-country through the woods,
to the tower on Hemlock Butte, where men we never saw
surveyed great tracts of green to find the faintest trails of smoke.

Since I was the smallest kid on the crew, I was always the one
to buckle on strap and spurs and climb, chopping branches on my way.
Thirty feet off the ground, I'd nail a ceramic insulator,
feed phone line through, and cinch it tight with wire on either side.

One morning in June our first tree of the summer stood across the road,
so I had to climb extra high to clear any log trucks passing by.
Spurs firmly set, knees shaking, I leaned back on the strap and surveyed
the vast forest stretching into blue Clearwater Mountains,
sunshine sparkling over the morning woods that came alive in me.

The big boys swinging axes would clear out brush under the line,
and then they'd pull it taut from below while I worked fast above.
I'd descend, and still wearing spurs, I'd fall over logs, blunder
down a brushy ravine, and splash through a creek to the next big tree.

Soon fire-fighting interrupted phone-line work, and we
never got the line restored—superseded anyway by short-wave phones.
As Virgil wrote in *Georgics* three, the best days are the first to flee,
but I am still perched high in that green day, poised to fly away.

Widow-Maker

Piling brush was deadly tedious work, detested by the crew.
Between forest fires, a week, a month, or all summer
we were trucked to clear-cuts, where only bone-white snags
and trees too small to take still stood among fresh stumps.

The rest was slash: broken bits of bark and branch scattered
when giant white pines and Douglas firs dropped through understory,
limbs lopped off and left where they fell—we dragged it all
and piled it high for foresters to set on fire when fall rains came.

Knee-deep in slash, bare-chested in bone-dry heat,
I was chatting with crew boss Art killing time on the skid road below.
Suddenly Art yelled, "Now that's what I call a widow-maker!"
High on a slope a hundred feet away a lofty snag began to tilt,
descending to earth in silent slow motion, crashing in a roil of dust.

We quickly scanned the other snags still standing all around us.
One gully over, the crew were building their own big pyres for the fall.
Larry shouted, "Bobcat!" and pointed down the ridge where she
picked her way through the naked mess we had made of her secret trail.

Leaving slash where it lay to enter the round of slow decay
would have served the forest well, but we were hired to clean the farm,
to make it convenient to harvest the next generation of clones,
as if our job were taming the earth until we no longer belonged.

New Work

Five a.m., a trucker throws open a steel door
as Portland starts taking the day's deliveries.
Headlights and thrumming engines fill the streets,
windows fill with light from inside office buildings.

Five p.m., we are witnessing the twilight of the last hundred years,
the fossil-fuel bingeing, slow-motion decline of what we know,
all the work it took to make farms big where no one lives,
machines rolling over petrochemical fields of terminator seeds.

Now we must turn our attention to what we can make by hand,
turn around and walk our way back to water and sun.
We must find equilibrium, an old garden we maintain,
turn our eyes skyward for signs of rain,
turn attention to the ground where life begins.

In the rainy wind of November the gardener makes compost
from leaves and vines that start their own banked fire,
steaming in the cold, becoming rich brown gold
the gardener feeds to plants that will in turn feed him.

In April grandchildren rush to help plant potatoes,
and then they know where potatoes come from, and how they grow.
The memory of this work will follow them through their days,
and the harvest we have been waiting for will have been there all along.

Julia and the Salmonberries

In June the earth discloses itself in flowers,
waiting for Julia to find them and call them by name: dead nettle
and the kind of nettle that she must touch to see if it really stings.
Of course it does, and then we find dock and self-heal.

We find foxgloves, which Julia's cousin Teagan called
"fox mittens," because he was too young to know what gloves are.
Julia laughs. I show her the salmonberry blossom,
the purple star that has been waiting just for her.

In July the berries assume their salmon-flesh complexion.
Julia discovers them and picks some, and in her cupped hands
they glow like little salmon suns, a clustered nebula of light,
reflecting Julia's dimpled face that beams with revelation.
She eats them one by one, declares them super delicious.

Don't they taste a little sour as other people say?
"I love sour things," says she, "I love salmonberries!"
Later in July, when only the top two foxgloves on every stem remain,
fruit receptacles, their berries gone, are left to wither away.

Will Julia forget what's no longer there? We often do.
What earth discloses always closes up again, like flowers,
nor can we hold in memory so many things revealed.
Everydayness rules, like the sun, passing behind a cloud.

Garden in Winter

Snow falls on Portland all day and all night,
ticking through fir boughs like a ghostly clock,
measuring out the shroud that covers the garden beds,
two feet deep and counting.

Beneath the bare branches of the pear tree
the compost pile settles and smolders.
Stone Amida Buddha assumes *dhyana mudra*
under a white mantle, dwelling on mystic fire.

Below the snow and subfreezing cold
Olympia winter spinach hibernates close to soil.
The Pure Land exists in every mind.
Winter spinach knows that sooner or later thaw sets in,
portending rebirth, bolting bright green.

Young Julia dancing along the garden path sings out,
"Hi Mr. Buddha, how are you today?"
Snow on his shoulders, Buddha says, "I am the same
as yesterday, and I will be waiting for you tomorrow."

Chinook winds rise like the cries of massed crows.
After the snow is gone, wan sunlight
accumulates on budding branches and brown earth.
Spring rain soon floods the garden paths again.

Sand Station

Fall came early to Portland, leaves gone in October.
I waved goodbye to my wife, who did not want me to go.
I knew by her face she'd already relapsed,
and I would find her adrift in isolation when I came back.

My stepfather had been disabled by a stroke,
leaving my mother oblivious, alone in Alzheimer's hold.
Called to arrange for her care, I was bound to go
seven hours upriver to Lewiston, Idaho.

After weeks of tending her and wrangling with siblings
to plan for long-term care, I left for Portland with no resolution.
I found myself stopping midway at Sand Station.
Overwhelmed by affliction behind and before me,
I banged my head on the steering wheel and cried.

I thought of Sand Station in summer, a shoreline strand
where families from Umatilla and Hermiston pitched tents.
Kiddies frolicked and screeched on McNary's artificial beach,
mommies and daddies barbecued under the sun.

Sand Station in October was empty, the shadow of death.
As night came on, I drifted off in darkness and isolation.
Beneath McNary's lake, still as the desert on either side,
a great river unknown to me was following the sun.

November

Bay View Motel at Russell Point on Coos Bay.
My dog Wolf, a black and silver miniature schnauzer,
sits on my lap at a window overlooking grey water and sky,
the beige dunes across the bay scarred by tracks.

Sometimes a seagull glides by on stiff wings,
or headlights drift across the Jordan Cove causeway.
Each time Wolf perks up for a better look,
a muted growl emanates from his throat.

As Wolf settles down and accepts seagulls and cars,
he renders total attention to water, sand, and sky.
I join him in his deep reverie, our animal synchronicity
merging in the wild mind before mind,
the way things are, have always been, and always will be.

The wind begins to raise a few whitecaps offshore,
and then a shower falls like strands of mist out of the clouds,
a black and silver curtain sailing east off the Pacific,
leaving in its wake a rainbow arcing over the bay.

Wolf sees through the world unfolding before him
the calm grey emptiness that makes the rainbow glow.
Striking out after him on November's cold and unknown shore,
I abandon consciousness and follow him past the horizon.

Fish Creek

for Mike Wiley

The midsummer creek fans out through small boulders
rounded and rolled by ancient migrations downstream.
Its waters enter the reticent Clackamas River
through trickling rills, a hundred anonymous mouths.

The longer we sit by the water, the more voices of fathers
whisper their sadness that catches in our ears,
like remote echoes of guilt from things done and left undone,
so only alluvial feeling descends to the sons.

Or maybe our memories masquerade as water,
and we hear from our fathers the guilt that we alone bear,
for water, the alchemists say, is our refining fire,
and what remains is what we have done and left undone,
the distant cries of children whose needs we can never redeem.

We can't help but see our father in ourselves:
His hands, his walk and his gaze converge in us
whenever we catch ourselves reflecting by the stream,
the way he stared into campfires by the rivers of our youth.

The Clackamas slides by in a slow, broad curve,
deepening here to a blue-green pool so clear
we can see old tires and hovering trout below,
silence absorbing the final murmurs of Fish Creek in its flow.

Rock

On Fish Creek Divide above the Clackamas River,
where second-growth fir crowds close to the road
and varied thrushes dart upstream into the brush,
autumn takes hold under clouds and constant rain.

Blocks of dusky andesite lie where they tumbled
down the escarpment of an old quarry,
shaped and cut by millions of years for men today
to pick natural bricks for garden walls.

Suddenly rain stops, clouds raise the horizon,
the king of the forest steps above the dripping terrain,
a mountain with snowy hair who unifies earth and sky.
Suddenly wind blows, clouds close in,
the king withdraws behind mist and rain.

Dark rocks fill the hands like wet mandalas,
shiny images of the Self, newly minted from ancient days,
lives of ancestors long-buried in forgotten places,
animal spirits who said things to women and men.

Down Fish Creek Divide on the Clackamas River,
a dipper flits from rock to rock in rough water,
then dives and disappears for long minutes,
only to reappear, somewhere downstream.

Abode of the Unplanned Effect

for Joe Stroud

Sun shines, apple trees bloom, leaves spring,
and we embark on a road trip along the Willamette,
finding the gravel track to Clem Starck's rustic estate
that he discovered in ruins and restored for Barbara and himself.

We wander Clem's acres of old oaks and new ponderosas,
Shiva racing ahead over the wild grasses,
until three turkey vultures gliding thermals of late afternoon
remind us that Charles waits in Corvallis.

On Crystal Lake Drive along the Willamette, Charles Goodrich
encountered an acre of land and built a house for Kapa and himself.
We four poets now sit around a table in the mud room,
drinking and laughing, conversation breaking into blossom,
like old friends meeting for the very first time.

Late at night we say farewell under crystalline stars,
touching invisible willows along the Willamette—
as you and I begin the long way back to the city of silence,
rolling through darkness on roads that are empty and still.

And if you should ask how I remember this trip,
we found the house of friendship and lingered there
like four leaves unfolding upon a single branch,
like green fire springing up into the bright air.

Death and the Mother

Midwinter night after steady rain and a strong gust of wind
the giant Douglas fir tore up its roots and fell.
Power lines flashed and sparked around the quivering branches,
the solid trunk so lightly laid upon the earth.

Older than the road she fell across, older than people living here,
she was soon chain-sawed by power-company men.
Above the upturned roots and resinous stump,
a great space had opened to the sky.

We mourned the loss of our lofty landlady
who sheltered us for thirty of her ninety years.
Jung says trees are unconscious symbols of the Mother,
like the one that Christ was hung upon,
And bisiden him stonden Marye and Johan.

Mother lay in a coma after her heart attack,
three days and nights wheezing behind an oxygen mask.
My sister whispered into her ear, "It's all right, Mom,
we love you, and you can let go."

When she stopped breathing, a great space opened to the sky,
as if a wind had suddenly swept everything out of its way.
Midsummer light lay gently in long beams across the fields,
and shoveled earth fell heavily into the grave.

Zürichsee

Carl Jung 1875–1961

An old woman pointed the way to Jung's tower,
ten minutes over a bicycle path along the train tracks,
past a sign extolling Bollingen's sandstone,
the "Shaman of Zürich" mentioned only in passing.

A guardian of the family trust filled the doorway,
demanding to know how we had found this place.
We said we had read Jung's life and work, and asked if we might go in.
"That depends," he said, and gave us a hard look.

He ushered us into the place the Shaman thought would outlive him:
The first dark tower, maternal hearth—where on April nights he heard
long-dead Swiss soldiers laughing and playing music on their march—
subsequent towers of spirit and ego, lake of the unconscious
rippling toward distant snowy peaks.

Within the tiny courtyard, Zürichsee lapping at our feet,
we studied the sandstone block carved by Jung:
Flanked by sun and moon, in clouds of Latin and Greek, the boy-god
roams the darkness like a star and points to the land of dreams.

We retraced our steps as numerous cyclists
passed us ringing their bells and singing out *"Grüß Gott!"*
We sat on a bench watching a sailboat tack across the lake
until it became a white speck against the far shore.

The Source of the Donau

At Donaueschingen we find the Donauquelle,
a round concrete pool that holds the original spring.
A statue pointing east portrays the Baar, the hills and valley here,
a child Donau at her feet and young man Donau beside her.

Thirteen hundred kilometers east the Donau
becomes Danubius, a middle-aged man in Budapest.
But here we relish lunch of wild boar in the Jägerstüble,
and ponder tributaries, in search of the one true source.

We follow the longest one, the River Breg, a rushing ditch,
up the mountain to Furtwangen and beyond.
A stone declares *Hier Entspringt der Hauptquellfluß der Donau—*
a piped spring bubbling below a soggy mountain meadow,
starting the Breg on its way to decrepit Sulina on the Black Sea.

Cold spring rain comes down, and near a tiny chapel of St. Martin
we find refuge in the Berggasthof, where a family feud is underway.
At a corner window overlooking the lush Valley of the Breg,
we drink coffee as voices from another room pour out.

That night at dinner in Hotel Falkon overlooking
the Black Forest resort at Baiersbronn, we share our table
with a businessman and his cross-dressing friend, who bubbles,
 "Dear heart, won't you pour me more of your sweet wine?"

Kraków, 11 September 2001

Inside static on the car radio, I hear the word *terrorysta*.
We enter our room at the Sofitel, where someone has left
the TV blaring, Twin Towers going up in smoke.
We hope it's science fiction, but we know it's American blowback.

The Brick Gothic asymmetrical towers of St. Mary's Basilica
have endured six centuries on Old Town Square.
Communicants press forward in Mass, the carved altarpiece
depicting the Death of Mary in a crowd of astonished apostles.

Leaving a shop on Stolarska Street known for morbid posters
boldly made by artists under the ghostly People's Republic,
we notice a line of solemn townsfolk bearing flowers and wreaths.
They are waiting to lay their sympathy and grief
at the door of the American consul across the street.

For the first time moved by the suffering in New York,
I pull out my camera and step between cars on Stolarska Street.
A policeman steps in front of me with one hand raised,
the other pointing at my camera, as if surveillance were mine.

Under the statue of Mickiewicz, I start to imagine Americans
will find within themselves the spirit of reconciliation
with those whose grievance has made such pain, but then
I see in Market Square the banner headline screaming: *terrorysta*!

Stary Zawidów

Jacob Böhme 1575–1624

We walk the bridge over the Neisse into decrepit Zgorzelec.
Jutta bargains with a Polish taxi driver who speaks a little *Deutsch*:
For twenty-five euros he will take us sixteen kilometers south
and wait while we look around, because, he says, "Waiting is free."

Jacob Böhme was born in a town he knew as Alt Seidenberg,
where generations of Böhmes had occupied most of the land.
His family home burned down in World War II,
when Germans were driven out and towns took Polish names.

Stary Zawidów rests on a bench of land above the Neisse.
A couple of dwellings remain among crumbling farm buildings,
encroaching greenery, and silence, the immense silence of God.
On the brow of the bench the ruddy spire of the church ascends,
once Catholic, Lutheran in Böhme's day, and Catholic once again.

Young Böhme apprenticed himself to shoemakers and traveled
Sachsen, Lausitz, and Böhmen, finding money and religion on his way.
Later he left the silence of God and walked sixteen kilometers to Görlitz,
city of noisy religious contention, and short on makers of shoes.

On Böhme's road north to Görlitz, the puzzled driver is asking,
"Do you want to find *Oma* or *Opa*? The *Friedhof* here is a nice place to see!"
We say we wanted to find where Böhme's fall and journey to grace began.
The driver shrugs. We do not say that waiting for God is free.

Grinzing

1991

Schubert and his friends in the generous spirit of spring
fled Vienna for old suburban villages like Grinzing,
where sprigs of pine or fir above the *Heurige* door
beckoned them to dance and sing, drink new wine.

One night on impulse Peter hailed us cabs for Grinzing,
to find fresh vintage for our own high spirits.
We strolled out to the wine-garden under linden trees,
the warm summer air festooned with glowing lanterns.

A modest wedding reception featured a man who sang
through a single amp that distorted his voice like sour wine.
We laughed, and we called this sodden party the dead wedding:
the groom so drunk he could barely stay on his chair,
the bride depressed, her father sitting apart from the rest.

Ingrid, lately resettled in the West after a life in the East,
still testy about bad manners and wretched excess,
asked the singer to desist, which buried the wedding completely.
Lo took offense at Ingrid's disdain, and Peter rushed off to call taxis.

After syphilis took hold, Schubert's longer bouts of depression
estranged his good-time friends—wine his final companion.
When Master Death asked him to leave his last symphony behind,
Schubert was only a drifter among the *Heurige* of Grinzing.

Perfectly Still

After a week of rain in May, I roll out my gas-driven mower
and roar back and forth across the overgrown greensward.
An hour later I put the mower away, and then I hear
what my mower had obscured: the racket of weed whackers,

leaf-blowers, and other mowers from neighboring yards.
Where did such technology come from and where
is it leading us now? Where did silence go, and when
will all the machines run down and let it return?

The weed whacker won't answer, but the blower blares on,
shoving clouds of debris from one side to the other.
The Empire spins away, like a dust devil in a desert,
lost in sheer immensity, the incommensurate scale.
Power runs down, and dust sinks back to earth.

My dog Wolf and I flee the lawns trimmed by noise,
take the trail to Marshall Park, the canyon of Tryon Creek,
left to go its own way. Under cedars and firs, we hear only water,
the silence of ten thousand leaves springing anew.

Here Wolf and I know what to listen for, the mute unknown
that lurks beyond our ken. A mallard in a quiet stretch
holds his place in time with the current, tilting his blue-green head,
scanning the creek bed as if it were sky, perfectly still.

Big Hole

Soldiers shot the old man checking on horses.
They charged the slumbering camp, gunning down
women and children, boot heel stomping the newborn.
Yellow Wolf said, "Some soldiers acted with crazy minds."

The *nimípu* called this meadow "place of ground squirrels,"
haven of willows and good grazing along the Big Hole River,
beyond the conflict with Idaho. No quarrel here with Montana,
the *nimípu* not knowing the whites were all of one mind.

One hundred thirty years later I walk the trail
to a skeletal village of lodge poles left behind.
Medicine bundles and bits of faded cloth dangle from ropes
placed by descendants of those who survived,
who yearly walk this trail under the August sun.

Screams of the slaughtered echo through time:
Mystic, Sand Creek, My Lai, Azizabad—unsuspecting villagers
caught sleeping or eating or playing out their common ways,
older than language or consciousness.

When will we Americans—crazy for all that we know—
stop projecting our own shadows and fears
upon indigenous people around the world?
Yellow Wolf said, "The air was heavy with sorrow."

Lochsa

Late August I come back to the Lochsa,
breathe the dry tang of cedar and goldenrod,
hear snowmelt rushing out of mountains
down the steep granite race to the Clearwater.

Summer afternoons of my youth along the river,
trout no longer taking the fly, I'd lay aside the rod,
recline upon some giant boulder midstream
and give my mind to the spirit of water.

Water foams over rocks in many voices,
transparent as air between two worlds,
falls silent in green pools that hold the dark enigma,
deeper than Ego can go, and I
let go on the current that carries all things away.

Summer nights camping along the river,
I'd hear distant voices whispering,
as body discovers the absence of mind,
as darkness falls behind closed eyes.

Now in late August I take photos of the Lochsa
at Nine-Mile Camp, photos no better than words
at showing this river running through my life
down the steep granite race to the Clearwater.

The Poem of Big Sur

The world is slipping away, falling into oblivion,
so only ghosts of places and their creatures linger here.
We must transform them all within our invisible hearts,
Rilke wrote, to make the world more present in us, to carry

things through time. Tumbling precipitously to sea,
Big Sur Mountains make a refuge meant to be
nowhere else on earth, uncanny blue water breaking white on rocks
like stones Jeffers hauled from Carmel Bay to build his poems.

The Big Sur poem is rugged enough to house a flock of condors,
nine-foot wingspans gliding coastal updrafts in lingering spirals.
Brought back like a dream from the edge of extinction,
the condor endures, as inside of us still lives
Homo erectus, eater of carrion, invisible after two million years.

Descending the trail to Smuggler's Cove, we hear the pebbly hiss
of North Pacific rattlesnake. Uncoiled and spooked,
he rears up and strikes twice, and fear hisses in our blood.
He slips away under cover of paintbrush and monkeyflower,

indigenous to the poem of Big Sur. At cove's mouth we spy
three sea otters calmly riding the swells, one snoozing on his back.
They don't sense they are endangered, but we do:
Our invisible hearts are home to otters now, and condors, and snakes.

Steptoe Butte

Detox two nights in Pendleton Red Lion.
We drove to Colfax and took the winding road up Steptoe Butte,
you queasy and unable to look down as world and time
slipped like ashen stubble fields toward distant mountains.

October 2007, Steptoe rides like a tall ship
a thousand feet above the ocean of burnt sienna swells
rolling under your feet like seasickness, your old life
dragged out of you, rising in your gorge like a rock.

Four hundred million years ago this quartzite pile
appeared on the coast of Pangaea's western sea,
later surrounded by waves of Columbia River basalt,
and twelve thousand years of swirling glacial dust.

In 1858 twelve hundred Palouse, Coeur d'Alene,
and Spokane rode ready to die down the hills of Pine Creek
to save their dwelling on earth from American desolation.
After one day's fight to retreat, dashing Colonel Steptoe
and his hundred fifty-two recruits fled under cover of night.

Thirty years later gregarious farmer James Davis,
called Cashup, because he always demanded cash,
built the road and a two-story hotel that occupied
the top of the butte, sixty by sixty feet.

In 1908, two boys set Cashup's dream on fire—
flames seen from every mountain, town, and farm
by old folks who were children then, dragged out of sleep
to witness Steptoe burning on the night's primeval sea.

We came home from Steptoe, and recovery has held.
Time and the world followed us back from distant mountains.
What happened before was blacked out,
but Steptoe Butte stays solid under our feet.

Greyhound Rock

My Idaho logo hat flew off my head and into the sea.
Receding wave pulled it just out of reach.
Suddenly I would have that hat back, no matter
if Greyhound Rock himself demanded it.

A second self in me rose up, assumed control,
all caution banished by pure intent, a focus to prevail.
I stepped up to my ankles in cold sea to grab that hat
riding the crest of a rising wave.

Suddenly wave swept the sand from under my feet.
I stood up sputtering, and next wave knocked me down again.
Joe saw panic on my face, but I felt a strange transcendent thrill.
I grabbed my drowned hat and crawled back to dry sand.
Only then I saw the wave had stripped the camera off my neck.

Perched on a rock, I saw the dead Nikon half-buried below.
As wave receded over it, I jumped in and grabbed the strap,
staggered out of the sea and hoisted it triumphantly,
as if I'd caught Leviathan, or a trophy of vision.

Joe photographed me grinning like a child.
An idle onlooker allowed he would've let the hat go.
Greyhound Rock, sea stack of Miocene mudstone, waits like a god
to strip the past from someone else, and send him back to shore.

Big Mosquito Lake

Gifford Pinchot National Forest

The water mirrors the late September sky,
stillness of snags and reeds along the shore,
short-branched firs awaiting loads of snow,
the pale Harvest Moon suspended in brilliant blue.

My son and I are older now since we first
spun our lines across the rushing Lewis,
letting flies drift along the current into eddies,
where rainbows break their sky for summer's last feast.

Since I last heard the boy's delight at holding his first trout,
he's become the father to his own son.
In them and every looking glass, I see my father's face.
We share with him the language of unmarked roads,
mountain forest and stream, where silence is supreme.

Now my son and I follow the shore of Big Mosquito Lake,
watching trout work the morning hatch,
mosquitoes big as crows, they say, attentive as dogs.
The old urge to cast a line rises and falls.

The hatch breaks off, still water returns,
and we fall into ourselves, dwelling on mystery's edge,
the moon above and the moon below,
the shared silence of men.

Wind Mountain

After climbing a mile of switchbacks and scree,
we come to rock pits built by Chinookan boys
who waited for spirit powers to show themselves,
reaching back to animal spirits we have always been.

The Columbia leads the eye in long and shining curves
toward the western end of the Gorge, Washougal
obscure in distant mist and darkness,
the way our vision cannot pass beyond death.

But here the mind turns to the absence of animals
in woods of starving second or third growth,
as if the world evolved only for humans,
a million more of us born every four days,
crowding the others into oblivion.

A thousand feet below, Wind River passes under
highway and railroad bridges to join the Columbia,
and Home Valley turns from farms to suburbia.
Trains and trucks pass through with horns blaring.

Our vision withdraws like the moon
as elk, bear, and eagle wait patiently within
for each of us to seek their spirits again,
for each of us to be ready to carry life forward on earth.

Agriculture

Asotin County was named after *nimípu* village *hasutin*
on the Idaho side of the Snake, *place for catching eels*.
On Washington's side the canyon slopes up to Columbia Plateau,
rolling hills of rich loess now devoted to winter wheat.

The Fitzgeralds ran a few head of cattle out of their ranch
up on Dry Creek, but mostly they farmed an acreage near Peola,
a defunct town just over the line in Garfield County.
The son called Fitz was fun to be with, always drinking and joking.

Once I asked his brother-in-law where Fitz got that limp.
Clarence explained how farmers used tractor-drawn machines
to inject liquid petroleum nitrates directly into the soil.
One day Fitz was horsing that stubborn machine into place,
when one of those injector knives stabbed him right through the foot.

"Ol' Fitz has limped like that ever since," Clarence gravely intoned.
Later, at the cabin near Peola, I walked out into a fallow field
overlooking the vast plateau rolling toward the Snake River Breaks
and picked up a pinch of dry, crusty grit that passed for soil.

Eventually agriculture fails. We take away more from earth
than we give back, humus abandoned in favor of chemicals.
After we no longer grow with oil, the young will have less to demand,
dwelling along the Snake, catching whatever they can.

November in Berlin

2008

Rain drips from sallow plane trees in the Tiergarten,
leaving rings upon the surface of the Neuer See.
Rusty oak and elm leaves on the verge of falling
hover over black waters that bear them away.

I re-enter the city's slow explosion of engines,
shoppers surging on the Ku'damm, headlines shouting
revelations of financial loss compounding
like concentric rings of a global tsunami.

At seventy-three Peter's knees give way to pain,
and Lo waits last on a list for a liver transplant.
As age gathers momentum toward the dark horizon,
Ingrid's cataracts reduce her driving to fits and starts,
and she refuses to celebrate her eightieth birthday this winter.

I wander the steel-and-glass government sector
rebuilt from ruins of World War II and communist neglect:
The glass-crowned stone shell of the Reichstag,
concrete stelae of the newly-demolished Palast der Republik.

Hollow-eyed intern of bylines and deadlines,
Anne lives out of her suitcase in Dresden and Berlin,
tells me she hates her laptop, her creativity circles the drain.
She has to believe that somewhere life is waiting for her.

Morning on the Neisse

Jacob Böhme, Master Shoemaker and citizen of Görlitz,
in 1600 at twenty-five beheld in a single flash
the blood-red birth of light and the two-fold structure of the world.
After twelve years' reflection, he wrote his first book, *Dawn*.

One morning in May we started across the new pedestrian bridge
to visit Böhme's house in Poland, the rose-colored one.
The border guard said only European citizens could cross,
so we made our way over the older bridge downstream.

Böhme wrote in *Dawn* that with the inner birth of soul
came the outer birth of evil, the shadow cold as air.
His cobbler's bench and his writing table stood where he left them,
overlooking the Neisse and St. Peter's Church on the opposite side.
As *Dawn* spread, the pastor ordered Böhme to stop writing.

We thought we could cross back over the foot bridge,
now that we had our passports stamped at the bridge below.
But no, the border guard said he told us already this morning:
Americans could not cross this bridge, not now, not ever.

After the second flash came to him from a pewter dish,
Böhme quit making shoes and wrote twenty-eight books in six years.
Exiled in Dresden, he was cleared of heresy, and back in Görlitz
He died writing *177 Theosophic Questions with Answers to Thirteen of Them*.

Baden-Baden

In Turgenev's novel the Russian expatriate rich and their sycophants
have nothing to do but chat in French and stroll the Lichtentaler Allee.
They fall in love and want to make Russia more like France,
but in the end their convictions go up in *Smoke*, and they all go home.

The beige band shell holds the orchestra like an antique pearl,
deftly wafting nostalgia over the white-haired invalids in folding chairs.
Strauss waltzes compete in spring with jaunty American tunes:
"Lovely weather for a sleigh ride together with you."

Dining on snails at Leo's, we notice a greybeard's shuffling small steps
of the late-stage alcoholic, baggy rumpled suit, and untucked shirt.
The concierge at the Steigenberger chirps, "Herr Reimann, how are we today?"
She straightens his tie. "*Nicht so gut*," he mumbles and sinks in a foyer chair.
Later he elevates to the upper floor, where the rich drop off in five-star luxury.

Lavish murals in Baden Casino's Florentine Room show ancient towns
serenaded by ceiling symphonies of cherubim and angels, framed
by five chandeliers, Baden coats of arms, and allegorical figures of prosperity.
A wheelchair man spins around the roulette tables, scattering chips like jewels.

Under warm rain we stroll the Lichtentaler Allee to Museum Frieder Burda,
to see the new show of mostly American twentieth century art: Warhol's
enormous portraits of Joseph Beuys, Marilyn Monroe, and Mao Zedong,
Anselm Kiefer's toy airplane speeding toward Twin Towers at dawn.

Afterlife

Friedrich Hölderlin 1770–1843

A sunny morning in Tübingen we flag a taxi to the yellow tower,
a replica built after the first one burned in 1870.
Declared incurably mad, the poet lived there thirty-six years
under the care of Herr Zimmer, the carpenter who locked the doors.

The Neckar slides by as muddy as in Hölderlin's day,
when his windows looked out on a meadow on the opposite bank.
He relished each spring's return with thousands of wild flowers—
the meadow now a shady park where confident families play.

Zimmer confiscated the poet's working papers, leaving him
nothing to do. Pacing his small round room, he fell inward,
talking to himself, and over the years light faded from his eyes.
Incoherence overcame his mind, and he could not finish a thought,
though he dashed off deft, impersonal poems, one on a piece of wood.

"When far the dwelling life of man into the distance goes,"
He wrote in his last lines, "then heaven's radiant height
Crowns man, as blossoms crown the trees, with light."
We dwell in dark enigma that allows our eyes to see.

The tower closes at noon, so we tarry on the medieval wall
overlooking pleasure boats tied up along the quay.
A light wind springs up, and somewhere from the town we hear
the creaking of a chain that holds a swaying sign we cannot see.

Todtnauberg

Martin Heidegger 1889–1976

We chase a thunderstorm into Freiburg after the rain.
By nightfall students roam the brook-lined streets,
drinking and yelling over techno-pop in the Augustinerplatz
until dawn breaks with banging trash cans and church bells.

After no sleep and strong coffee, we find our way south
to the High Black Forest, where Martin used to flee Freiburg
to work on *Being and Time* in the cabin Elfride had built for him,
until their noisy children forced him to take a room at a farm.

The village of Todtnauberg spills below a small white chapel
down a steep slope, the southwestern flank of the Feldberg.
Time ends for each one of us on this mountain.
Passing beyond existence, we leave the living our messages
like shadows of clouds passing over green meadows.

Up here the air is strong, and a man can breathe the way he should.
Farmers waved to Martin striding down the mountain
to rejoin his colleagues in Freiburg's fetid atmosphere.
Martin waved back like a man who had died in his sleep.

We follow the setting sun into Freiburg, the students gone,
small streams sluicing through silent streets. Next day
we follow Martin to his grave on a hill at Messkirch.
The white chapel is waiting for us, and the uncanny stillness at noon.

Willow Tree

"Why are there beings at all instead of nothing?"
Heidegger cleared his throat. "That is the question."
In early December a violent wind twisted the half-rotten
fifty-year old willow off its roots and hurled it to the ground.

Memories lived like toadstools around that tree, where kids
played house and hideaway on summer days. The fallen trunk
carried a rusty hoop, the nailed base long overgrown.
The crotch gave up a plastic yellow phone that no longer rang.

The willow stood unique in our neighborhood, complete,
still in its downward sweep, unchanging and wholly present.
A small girl stopped and said, "This is my favorite tree."
Ice storms came, and branches fell, but always in spring
the willow glowed light green, assuming its graceful form.

After it fell, a woodcutter came and wanted to buy
the willow for firewood, so I gave it to him for nothing.
Chain saw and splitting maul dismembered branch and trunk,
left a thousand willow twigs, in Chinese poems a sign of departure.

I chopped up and wheeled away root and hollow stump.
I leaned on my ax and studied the space the willow once occupied,
now a smattering of sawdust in the dirt.
Without question, nothing would remain.

Rough Water

for Joe and Tim Stroud

Rain and snow-melt tear the river bed out of granite,
creeks tumble down steep slopes no glacier has carved.
The Lochsa holds its downrush against the rising ground,
foaming over boulders, the dark slumber of Earth.

Hordes of mosquitoes relentlessly seek blood,
deer's head orchids open, a single morel stands up.
The upper half of a deer skull lies where it fell,
molars bone-white against the bright green leaves of June.

The Lochsa of my youth was never this high, but always fast,
slowing around boulders where I could wade and fish.
Earth is like a stone that is no different broken open.
Earth shelters us but withholds itself unless
we suddenly see it unconcealed, before it closes up again.

Below the confluence of Lochsa and Selway Rivers,
we encounter the rarest wildflower: the phantom orchid.
It holds no chlorophyll, rising bone-white without leaves,
a ghost from an unmarked grave, standing up before it disappears.

Under summer sun the Lochsa dies down, boulders emerge,
goldenrod and yarrow bloom along the highway.
By then we have moved on, gone underground
like broken stones embedded in the dark slumber of Earth.

Finding My Grave

Lewiston, Idaho

My old companion November comes to Memorial Gardens,
ruddy dogwood and golden ash glowing over the lawn.
Under a wan sun, smoky haze shrouds stubble fields
where geese gather as if to plan their long migration.

As humans house their dead before they house themselves,
the grave I am destined to find has always existed.
The same plot where mother and father lie buried
has room for the child who returns to original ground.

In youth I roamed these fields in wheat or in stubble,
south towards Waha Mountain, tamarack there going yellow now.
Endowed by death, I travel the earth, but yearly come home,
remember my dead, linger beside their bronze names,
renew the meaning of being alive.

Accepting the fact of my death, I had not imagined
the place that would resolve my sojourn on earth
would welcome me to join the density of the dead,
the patience of sleepers waiting to be born.

Soon rain will sweep the haze from fields plowed for winter wheat,
and geese long gone over Waha Mountain begin their return.
Like some green pine, I find a relief beyond knowing:
Here is the place I began, and here is the place I am bound.

Clackamas Lake

for Mike Wiley

We pass through the August arch over Pacific Crest Trail,
cathedral door to Romanesque Douglas fir and Gothic hemlock.
People project holiness on ancient forest where none exists:
a concentration camp where trees try to wait us out.

Beyond the trees we see the reedy expanse of Clackamas Meadow.
We imagine its meandering brook as habitat for bull trout
our fathers once caught, now long gone from empty waters in Idaho.
A tiny cabin sits on the edge of the meadow with no one in it.

We come to springs bubbling from underground and flowing
across the lake as blue as sky into a fork of the Clackamas River,
and so on down to Pacific Ocean. We talk about our projections of God
over place and time and mind. But is projection such a big surprise?
Don't we already know who God is?

At the campground some of the six billion people on earth
have spread their plastic gear next to their cars in numbered spaces.
We hike outside the barbed wire fence that defines their realm and calms
their fear of any animals still at large, like bandits from the hills.

The dusty trail emerges from the forest to cross the asphalt,
where we encounter a toothless couple selling firewood.
They say they don't walk anymore, but only drive their car.
God is you, and God is me, and God is the hush when night falls.

Strangers

Marshall Park, Portland, March

Tryon Creek turns milky and swollen after a month of rains.
As my dog Wolf and I pick our way down the muddy trail,
we meet Randy from LA, doubting his cell phone's direction.
He joins us because we already know the trail to Lancaster Road.

Randy says he's ignorant of the forest around us.
I point out nettles just now rising from the mud bank
through newly emergent creeping buttercup.
Randy asks me again which is nettle, which is buttercup.

Presences of plants elude us, like small creatures lurking
inside blackberry thickets when Wolf pricks up his ears.
We live within the world, and we hide it from ourselves.
Trilliums bloom like wandering stars against the duff,
and osoberry leaves rest on bare canes like a flutter of green butterflies.

Randy brandishes a damp branch to ward off mountain lions,
because there are cougars in LA, and don't we have them here?
I say he is more likely to meet coyote or deer, and even then
only by chance, because they hide themselves from us.

What do we need to know about the earth wherein
we already dwell? We follow our cell phones through time
with no clear answer on the other end. Randy admires the moss.
Purple salmonberry blossoms are nodding in the sun.

Replanting Peas

for Lars Nordström

As any good gardener around here knows,
last year was the worst year for gardens in memory:
A wet spring followed by a wet June and a cloudy
damp summer left tomatoes still green in September.

This year twenty-eight days of rain in March
rotted my peas in the ground, just as Lars predicted.
Lars is building a new greenhouse, and doggedly I replant peas.
Under relentless April rain, new peas circle the drain.

Dwelling on earth, we cultivate water and soil,
as if we are always building a greenhouse for ourselves.
When we build we dwell, and we cultivate when we build.
Good harvest depends on reliable weather year after year,
as though each of us were given one small field on earth.

Lars, pruning and tying his vines, reminds me weather
goes in cycles: Growers in France before the war lost grapes
three years running, and everyone deplored the dearth of wine.
Lars says mildew claimed his Phoenix vintage just last fall.

What if our wetter seasons signal climate change,
when higher global degrees cause loss of ice, more water in air,
sending one storm after another scudding over us from the sea?
Growers of grapes and peas will be the first to know.

Turning Compost

Mid-September I pull the cord on my Tomahawk,
a roaring 8-horse chipper nobody makes anymore.
Over a month its spinning flails reduce a mountain of brush
to a few wheelbarrows of chips, as hungry blue jays shout.

Late October I mow up magnolia, maple, and alder leaves,
pile them over the chips, sprinkle a handful of nitrogen,
and just add water to ignite the slow invisible fire,
the whole pile steaming under November frost.

A sunny day in January I fork apart *nigredo*,
compost gone cold in damp decay, and smell the sweet
dark matter of mystery, root of all that grows.
I make a mound of chips and a mound of leaves,
and then I break for lunch, for an hour, for a day.

I rebuild the pile: layer of leaves, layer of chips,
a little nitrogen and water every three layers or so.
The re-ignited pile begins to steam and sink
under flurries of February snow.

Middle of March I fork the first wheelbarrows
of dense and juicy compost from the loaf.
I spread it over garden mounds for spuds, lettuce, onions, peas.
Robins whistle and bumblebees hum over humus reborn.

Night Music

After 99 years, his mother decides she no longer wants to live.
She will not leave her bed. She turns her face to the wall.
Morphine breaks over her pain like waves of oblivion.
She suffers more than we want to know.

A girl wakes up in a wavering hallway.
At the far end a door opens to boundless darkness.
Voices whisper, "Can you see us?"
Her fear is more than we want to know.

Night conceals, like the mind that no longer recalls
times when memories were made.
Hurtling toward winter's still moment, we
add minutes like bits of night to each day. Old guilt
about mothers and children rises from graves that night opens.

Yellow leaves twirl one by one to earth.
By morning the tree is bare as a hearse after the funeral.
Fog approaches the suburbs like a soft wall.
Emptiness foretold cancels everything we know.

As evening dies, we hear the voices of children.
We cannot tell if they suffer or play.
Their brittle screams twirl one by one to earth.
Parentless as gypsy moths, we wander the forest of night.

Green Chain

In *The German Ideology* Marx wrote that we produce ourselves
through labor. My last summer working in the Lewiston mill,
I was posted to the Extra Board, so I could be called
day or night for any available shift or particular job.

I did all kinds of jobs, including two weeks of graveyard
inside a dusty sweltering tower atop the stacker,
jumping down, laying out strips of lath, then hopping
out of the way before the next layer of boards rumbled down.

Green chain was feared by all of us on the Extra Board.
For a straight-eight hour shift we stood beside the chain conveyor
jerking four-by-eight-foot sheets of plywood, oozing wet,
onto platform carts, slamming the iron stanchions with a clang.
Green chain sometimes brought us long wet boards heavy as God.

My father believed hard work built character in his kid,
so he picked me up at the mill gate, grinning like morning sun.
Every cell in my body screamed with pain, my arms hung on the car seat
like pounded meat, my brain bruised with exhaustion.

Even then I knew I was only a temporary tool,
and some day most jobs on the Extra Board would be done by machines.
Green chain was so hard, we were not expected to live.
If labor was how I produced myself, I wanted a different job!

The Golden Bird

To put myself through college, like many sons of the Company,
I worked three summers at the lumber mill in Lewiston.
The box factory ripped short boards into smaller blanks, mostly for toys.
My job was to collect them from the saw and stack them on pallets.

The master of the bench saw was an old-timer called Tex.
That wasn't his real name, but everyone knew him as Tex.
Under the racket of saws and rollers, Tex never said a word,
but he could raise an eyebrow, and you knew exactly what he meant.

One summer I came home from San Francisco State stoked on Yeats.
I carried his typed-out poems to memorize on breaks:
The whine of saws would die away, and I, like some toy bird
made of hammered gold, would sing in a low hum:
I have sailed the seas and come / to the holy city of Byzantium.

Back at work on my side of the bench, my hand almost skimmed
the screaming blade. Tex stopped work and glared.
He held up his board-pushing hand with two stubs for ghost fingers.
He shook his head, picked up a board, and went back to work.

When the mill whistle blew at quitting time, Tex and the other men
would rush from the factory almost on a run. O let me linger
a moment longer in that long-gone summer out of time,
humming from my golden bough of all the poems to come.

Rincon Annex

Summer 1968

Off the east end of Market Street the depot where I sorted mail
occupied a city block on Rincon Point in San Francisco Bay.
Its square three stories built in Streamline Moderne
about the time I was born had gone a dirty grey.

Within cavernous rooms painted institutional green,
night clerks sat before sorting boxes flipping letters by zone,
their faces pale as zombies under flickering fluorescence.
New sorting machines would someday replace us all.

Shortly after I started in June, Sirhan Sirhan shot Bobby Kennedy.
After JFK, Malcolm X, and King, assassination canceled hope like a letter.
In that dreary summer of discontent and death, we were paid in grief.
In August Soviet tanks crushed the crowds of Prague Spring,
and Mayor Daley's cops attacked protestors in Chicago.

On breaks, clerks lounged under Rincon's dolphin motif on Spear,
passing joints along the line. Coming down from methedrine,
clerks with vacant eyes, missing teeth, and thinning hair
found death's second self on Rincon's roof in piles of mail sacks.

Back at work, too stoned to sort, I got myself assigned to postcards,
so I could ponder coastlines of the world, Mediterranean towns,
Kodachrome scenes where dreams go on vacation. As sun rose gold
over the Bay, I drove away over San Francisco's long Embarcadero.

Cathlapotle: The Pestilence

Clark drifting downstream in eighteen-five
reckoned three hundred people in fourteen lodges.
Heading upstream the year after, he counted nine hundred,
so many relatives assembled for the run of spring chinook.

Sited where three rivers meet, Cathlapotle flourished,
trading wapato, fish, canoes, and slaves,
dwelling in cedar lodges planted on the flood plain,
protected by houseposts of bare-ribbed ancestors.

One midsummer day the intermittent fever came.
People shivered, sweated, and threw themselves in rivers
to flee the tiny darts of death, and still they died.
Cathlapotle empty, starving dogs along the river
howled among corpses at summer's end.

Sited where two rivers meet, Portland flourishes,
selling timber, silicon, property, and labor,
dwelling in single-family units perched on hillsides,
protected by pavement, good drainage, and special destiny.

Klickitats took over Cathlapotle, and they died soon
or drifted away, disbanding to the Yakama Reservation,
so many dead, and dying again, that no one ever counted them.
Cathlapotle reverted to alders, nettles, and rain.

November Light

Noontide sunlight falls at the same low angle
as the restored roof planks of the house at Cathlapotle.
They almost touch the earth. The limbs of an old Oregon oak
splay like bronze wings, almost touching the earth.

As we approach the marshy lake, a nutria's blunt nose
spreads the water behind in a wide V.
Six scrub jays argue over the last bugs of autumn.
The girl makes a song: "Happy, happy blue jays!"

The girl cannot see birds with her binoculars.
We creep to a rock outcropping overlooking a wetland.
A flock of white egrets bursts skyward like winter light.
A kingfisher perches on the topmost branch.
The girl cannot see it through her binoculars.

We come to a slough where blue herons are standing.
Geese rapidly surge by in a sideways V.
On a distant pond ducks splash each other for space.
The girl makes another song: "Happy, happy ducks!"

Crossing the bridge, we see the yellow trees
reflected upside down in the stillness of Lake River.
They are nested beneath the dark window of earth.
Geese rise in a concert of wings, to follow the calling light.

Lownsdale Square

At noon the citizens on jury duty
issue from Multnomah County Court
to mingle with office workers and retail clerks
lunching and reading on benches.

Hundred-year-old elms extend their arms,
shading the square from the sun of mid-July;
a preacher takes up his station off to one side,
prepared to shout down traffic on Fourth and Salmon.

A soldier upon a pillar for the sixty-four Oregonians
who fell in the Philippines a century ago
occupies the center of the square to mark the first
American Indian-fighting expedition overseas—
a hundred Oregonians dead in Iraq so far.

"You there, walking away,
you're guilty as sin and you better get right with God—
or you're going straight to hell!"
shouts the preacher at no one in particular.

Under delicate gingko trees
the fountain in the middle of Main
spews water into troughs for ghost horses;
a bronze elk surveys the lawn where real elk once grazed.

Sleepers

Grandparents and granddaughter doze restlessly in one room.
The dog lies curled beside them on the empty tundra of sleep.
Wind drives the full moon across the sky as dreams
struggle to the surface in a grimace or an unclenched hand.

Ash trees are rigid flames in autumn's twilight.
Girls playing soccer kick the moon through an empty frame.
Rain sweeps over Mt. Sylvania and dimples the asphalt,
the street a black river the sleepers cross to oblivion.

On the far side someone is stalking them, and so they run
for what seems forever, but really only minutes pass.
The sleepers can do nothing but flee, or wait for light.
Then they are falling, tumbling like dry leaves through darkness
driven blind, no destination, no direction.

In a second growth forest, under a shroud of moss
a Volkswagen decays, and ivy envelopes a blue house.
The girl dreams of kicking the moon through the wrong goal.
Human dominion is left out in the rain.

Grandparents and grandchild sleep like the dead in their tomb.
The dog starts up as if to answer a distant call.
Wind drives the full moon out of a cloud, and silver light
builds ghost forests and ghost houses for the missing generation.

April Rain

for Jutta Donath

Twilight showers trickle down the dark window,
where flames of candles quiver upward in reflection.
Sustained tones of Albinoni's adagio pool in the room.
We sit down at our old oak table for dinner at home.

We eat potatoes stored since last September,
spinach salad from winter garden, and warm soup
stocked with overwintered leeks, carrots, sprigs of parsley.
How romantic, we agree, to have grown it all ourselves.

Our journey through time persists in this place,
where we have built a way of living. Children gone,
two people remain, and simple oneness prevails.
This table is the center of the house, and no one but we
occupy these chairs, assigned to us before we arrived.

April rain means planting new potatoes and peas.
Grandchildren come and swarm freshly turned mounds,
seed in hand, learning thumb-and-finger-drill,
until a sudden squall sends them to their screens indoors.

Dwelling in one place is how earth wants us to be,
the full moon says, filling the window with unearthly light.
Albinoni seems to agree, the oboe dancing sweetly into silence.
Candles burn down and so do we, embraced by all that we are.

Weimar Cantata

"The White Swan welcomes you with open wings,"
wrote Goethe, inviting a friend to stay next door.
Twenty years after we first came to Weimar, we find ourselves
an outside table under the sign of Gasthaus zum weissen Schwan.

We notice five street urchins chasing over the cobblestones
around the iron Goethe Fountain and out of sight along the Frauenplan.
Sunlight sparkles briefly in glasses of water and white wine
as evening settles down behind the linden trees.

Back in the days of DDR, we could afford a night in Hotel Elephant,
where Bach's house stood during his nine-year stay.
Today a music-student adagio is wafting over town like a revenant dream.
Here Bach conceived his best-known sons, Wilhelm Friedman, C. P. E.,
and all six Brandenburgs, those ageless, contradancing melodies.

We wander along the River Ilm under Austrian pines
to the white statue of Liszt, whose wide hands made pianos sing.
Kindergarten children frolic at his feet as daughter Cosima once did.
His fixed inspired stare flies far over their heads.

Like paired swans, we follow our close and intimate way,
gliding through the stillness of twilight, savoring time.
Twenty years after we first came to Weimar, we find our love redeemed,
find ourselves serenely adrift upon the vast mysterious stream.

Envoi: Rowena Crest

for Michael McDowell

College students in Hood River wonder why we keep writing
and publishing poems when no money can pay for time so spent.
We glance at each other, and I reply that poetry is a gift,
and when we are given that gift, we have to keep giving it back.

Later we drive upriver to Rowena Crest, McCall's sanctuary.
We walk the bench above Rowena Dell, where yellow balsamroot
blooms like clusters of brown-eyed suns, spinning in the breeze.
A Columbia Gorge squall falls upon us, splattering rain.

From the Crest we see the bare Gorge walls, the kolk lake in Mayer Park,
and Lyle gravel bar—all left behind by Bretz Floods thirteen thousand years ago.
We hope for poems that resonate what is, the way basalt echoes place and time.
The Klickitat River flows through lava walls scoured by the same
Bretz Floods, its narrow stream a primeval salmon run.

Back in McCall's refuge, before the next Gorge squall,
you photograph the purple lupine on the verge of Rowena Dell.
In momentary stillness they stand like hieratic pine cones
holding their place in time, ageless and serene.

We keep on waiting for poems, for only poems keep being alive.
They reveal the ancient round of balance lost and restored.
To those who follow we hand over the past that poems recall:
yours about dead Memaloose, mine about the ghost Celilo Falls.

About the Author

Bill Siverly was born and grew up in Lewiston, Idaho, and he has lived in Portland, Oregon, since 1972. He holds a Master of Arts degree from San Francisco State University. He taught Native American and world literatures, composition, and creative writing at Portland Community College for twenty-five years. Bill has published four books of poems: *Parzival* (1981), *Phoenix Fire* (1987), *The Turn* (2000), and *Clearwater Way* (2009). Since 2002 he has been co-editor with Michael McDowell of *Windfall: A Journal of Poetry of Place*, which features poetry of the Pacific Northwest and appears twice yearly on the equinoxes.

Colophon

Titles and text are set in Bodoni, a typeface designed by Giambattista Bodoni in 1790 and updated in 1926 by Heinrich Jost. The book is printed in a limited edition.